TIBERIUS AT THE BEEHIVE

TIBERIUS AT THE BEEHIVE

Kevin Ireland

Illustrated by Malcolm Walker

Auckland University Press

First published 1990
Auckland University Press
University of Auckland
Private Bag, Auckland

ISBN 1 86940 043 7

Publication is assisted
by the New Zealand Literary Fund
of the Queen Elizabeth II Arts Council

Typeset in Palatino
and printed by University Printing Services,
Auckland

Distributed outside New Zealand
by Oxford University Press

To Gita, Marjorie, Clare,
Vipsania, Julia

Tiberius Claudius Nero (42BC–AD37, Emperor AD14–37) was a far more complex political figure than the tyrant and libertine of popular history. He was a shrewd commercial administrator, a ruthless manipulator, and a natural leader, but the combination of opportunist mind, suspicious pride and the precariousness of his early life, followed by the isolating nature of his position as Emperor, left him with an indifference towards individuals and a fierce, distrustful contempt for underlings. Tiberius was also one of history's great exiles, spending two long periods of his life observing events in Rome from Rhodes and Capri.

The 1980s saw two intuitively gifted, gloriously larger-than-life New Zealand Prime Ministers go into political exile, though both retained observer status at the 'Beehive'. It seemed that the faction-ridden plottings of Roman politics had revived in the Antipodes, and that the head of state had become a new Caesar — of whim, favour, improvisation, superstition, and disdain. The poems consider the Tiberius of old and the composite phantom who carried out his most recent imperial policies.

K.I.

Contents

1 Political gossip

Political gossip has the Emperor
taking early retirement
to regain an appetite for power.

That's a new one. Last week he'd seen
a ghost. Keep listening. Keep guessing.
Or why not take a good rummage

through the entrails of a chicken?
Blood and guts are rich in rumour
and have other unique satisfactions:

they please the Gods, they fill
the ears of the deaf with echoes
and they are charged with the most

delicate disgust. Everyone
gets something out of them.
Except the chicken.

2   The name of the place

The House of Parliament,
yet they call it the Beehive.

Names tell us so much
about the givers of names.

Nothing could better signify
our press, our officials,

and the senators
than the way they took to it.

Sometimes I lie here
on my island retreat

and fancy I catch the stink
of them. A thin

diabetic scent of honey.
And remember golden smiles,

dancing signals,
buzz, buzz,

the viscid dribble of their praise.
Yet the name of the place

always owed less to its product
than the fear of my sting.

3 A tour of Parliament

I owned this building once.
It was my slit-visored helmet,
my pin-striped waistcoat,
a turnip-watch I wound with a caress,
a shopping-bag, a fat wallet,
a knobkerrie, a gaming wheel.
It was my tame toad.
It was my honey-pot, my hive.

The windows gazed inwards on me.
The concretework jutted as taut
as knuckles in a surgical glove.
The doors opened to you all as easily
as my smile. The suck of their closing
was the last syllable of my final word.

4 An old man on Capri

There is nothing that amuses me more,
so far from the Forum, in my decline,
than to torture the politicians

with the prospect of my return.
Of course, I take pleasure also from wine
and food, and the occasional boatload

of Assyrian virgins, plump and glossy
as a basket of dates, but making
the senators sweat is my favourite treat.

They were born with respect for the boss
and I'd hate them to lose it. Aching
for the whip gives them a sense

of things better than themselves,
a higher purpose in life. I used to go
to great pains — myself — to tell them

how little I liked flogging dead horses,
then sit back, chew grapes and watch the slow
lash of truth water their eyes.

5 Forgetting

My books engineer the records so that
you may forget. Past events change
more rapidly than your worst imaginings.

History is too flimsy and untrustworthy
to keep dreams safe. I am not going
to accommodate my purposes to such risks —

it makes better sense to write certainties so that
my truth cannot be deformed. Forgetting leads
the way: it straightens out the kinks,

sweeps away the clutter of technicalities.
It leads the assault on the treacheries
of the archives. It demolishes doubt,

obliterates contradiction, blots out disrespect.
Forgetting is the entrance to the new order.

6   Caesar eaten

They keep asking why I left Rome,
why I live aloof from the crowd.

Well, I have suffered years
stuck in their schools, armies

and assemblies — bogged down
in their debates — splattered

with rhetoric. Their yabber
was mud in my ears.

And as the words squelched
round me I saw nothing

but mouths. Appeals, entreaties,
demands and lies, lies, lies.

Open mouths — ovals and circles —
bawling, pleading, howling.

The lips set with bangles
of teeth. Bracelets of merciless,

devouring teeth. When God
looked out upon the multitude

He noticed first the eyes,
goggling with greed.

Then He saw the teeth.
They swirled about Him like shoals

of tiny, silvery fish.
Piranha teeth.

God's next act
was to move to higher ground.

7   A dark dry rain

I have made an arrangement with history
to go down as the King of Debauchery.

It wasn't always the treat you'd think.
It was sometimes a laugh, more often

a chore. Dissipation wins gold laurels
but takes a toll. To keep up the part

I became a secret reader late at night.
Often I stood at a window

and gazed at the stars. A lost man.
Haunted. Obsessed. Then I found her —

the goddess — a woman I passed
one day in the street. She was staring

sideways and up. My chariot brushed her,
yet she neither flinched nor turned.

Something distracted her. A bird? The shape
of a cloud? I looked into the skies. A dark

dry rain of sharp stones battered my eyes.
It stripped my sockets and ground

into my heart. Rock rasping on rock.
Each day I search for her. That ecstasy

of milled bone, gashed flesh and blindness.
I call it love. Sometimes I am sure I see

her in the distance. I run and shout.
She is always out of my reach.

8   Paper and ink

The distractions of office
are the chief complaint
of those frivolous enough
to imagine them. The quaint

notion that some shallow
abstraction could interpose
itself between my character
and my deeper purposes

amuses me. My attention never
wanders, I do not dry-dream.
How could I be rattled
by reveries? What may seem to some

to be, say, an absent-minded
scratch in my toga, an attack
of boredom, is finical vigilance.
I chase fleas to track

the dogs that bring them. The trouble
is that a rake through my sleeves
may shake out libraries
of proclamations, sheaves

of edicts, blizzards of forms.
I have become a body of statutes.
An executive God.
A king in a paper suit.

When I look at my hands
after I've given my skin a rub,
the sight speaks volumes.
They demand a good scrub.

For one thing, I collect ink
under my nails. The mud
of office. The citizens, however,
often mistake it for dried blood.

9 Law and order

They accuse me of crimes.
That's a laugh. My first principle
in politics is the maintenance
of law and order.

The streets are swept,
offices open on time,
the people are cheerful.
How does this tie in

with tales of executions,
dragging my victims on hooks
down the stairs of Parliament,
heaving them off the tops

of government buildings?
Liberals count corpses
whenever a train runs on time.
But it doesn't happen like that

in the modern state.
Tiberius has no need to shed blood
when his enemies imagine
such appropriate punishments.

10 Cards of identity

The idea seems to be getting about
that small odds and ends of numbered plastic
carried in the handbag or pocket curtail
your precious liberty. Well, so far

as criminals, bludgers, free-loaders,
frauds, bigamists and illegal immigrants
are concerned, I suppose you could say
I intend to restrict their freedom

to welsh, sponge and sneak off the rest
of the community. My joke on the platform
is to call them curs. 'Curs!' I cry.
'I'll tail them, all right! They need

curtailing, and they'll get it!' It never
fails to get a laugh and a cheer. It gets
the slobs in the right mood for the next
piece of wisdom, which always runs: cards

of identity protect the truth — honest
men and women have nothing to fear —
as documents dismantle your sum and substance
and data banks split your particulars

think how you are disencumbered —
everything is laid bare — there are no mysteries —
you have no guilty secrets — no private cares —
no ghosts — you are safe from betrayal.

11 Political friendship

The day you get to the top
the first thing you always do
is lock the door, lean back

in the number one chair and flop
your feet on the desk. A moment
in private to relish your triumph.

But the minute you're comfortable
you hear a sound like rain.
A quiet tapping. Then insistent.

Tap, tap, tap. Louder and faster.
A tropical downpour. It's your backers,
your allies and intimates — knocking.

They want to get in to congratulate you
and remind you of their support,
and wish you well —

and beg just one small favour.
It's never for themselves.
They wouldn't be so insensitive,

so mercenary. Always — the first
time they ask — it's for somebody else.
A deserving case. Another good friend.

12   Radiant particles

Personality or magnetism won't do.
Aura is the word I'm looking for.

It surrounds me in a field
of radiant particles so small

they are invisible to the eye —
yet blinding. No one can look on me

without wincing. They are dazzled.
It is like staring at the sun.

Sometimes I switch myself off,
just to test the reaction.

Who is this fat runt,
they ask themselves, this nobody?

I can read their disbelief,
their disappointment. Then,

without warning, I turn the juice
back on again, observe the shock.

They are scorched by lightning.
Thunder bursts their eardrums.

My face is a new-minted golden coin.
It blazes above them. King Pig.

13   Listening to the radio

Their voices uplifted him
with their irritable debates,
sullen ramblings,
and ratty little tiffs.

He would hug himself
the more the arguments
broke down into bickering
and points of order.

Nothing pleased him more
than to hear two of them
scratch at each other
like fagged-out toddlers.

As they improvised insults,
snapped, crackled,
niggled and twangled,
Tiberius turned up the static.

It gave him great joy
to listen to them prove
his slogan: Dictatorship Loves You —
Democracy Hates.

14   The idleness of poets

You call it a poet's dream?
Island in the sun
with all mod. cons?

Nothing to do but reach out
for what you want, or feel
you should or might?

But I don't chew lotus leaves.
Plain food, good booze — that's all
I need. Plus a few books,

a girl or two, pink and hot
from the bath, and no worries.
A poet's *dream*?

I call it Everyday Life.
It's the working model for my plan
for our old age pensioners.

I don't see anything sybaritic
in living like this.
There's nothing degenerate about it.

I'm a sort of God of Social Services,
Emperor of Popular Welfare.
I can choose what I like

from the treats and not bother
about the rest. Nobody forces me
to enjoy myself. And you don't

catch me writing poems
about it either. It would make me feel
I wanted to escape from here

if I wrote messages, shaped them
into pages and sailed them away
into the future like paper boats.

15   Caesar in the bath

They are not real boys
or girls in my bath.
The shadows you see

slipping about the deep end
could be jellyfish, squids,
eels. They are playthings.

Flopping around in a bath
gives me the same enjoyment
that you would get

from reading a good book.
Think of them: the silver sacs
of round vowels snagging

in the hairs of your legs,
the consonants wobbling
and spiralling,

words seething whenever
you kicked your feet
or dived. A small bubble

just slid up my thigh.
For a moment I thought it was
a finger. Look down between

my knees. The children's faces
are only mosaics, memories.
Nothing in a bath is real.

I splash, and my reflection
fractures. Ripples dismember me.
My smile scuds like a shoal

of sprats to a marble wall
as white as a breaking wave.
Foam stabs out my eyes.

The word for this is pleasure.
It pops and crackles
as it hits the surface.

16   Enemies of state

The infection seems to be spreading.
It's just the right time for some of you
to get out of town and sniff the warm winds

of Capri. I especially recommend the breeze
at the top of the cliffs. I'm serious.
Illness disgusts me. I never joke about it.

And this one's a particularly nasty epidemic.
It takes no account of age, sex,
or status. You go to bed feeling fine,

then wake in the morning with a fit
of conscience — that's the first sign.
By midday you're in a fever of reform,

and by evening we have another festering,
suppurating enemy of state. Streets
turn away from you. The city forgets you.

The stars no longer concern themselves
with your fate. Your name decomposes. Your past
dies. Officially, you have never existed.

The best cure is the trip I suggested.
The cliffs take your mind off contagions.
Look out to sea and contemplate flying.

17 A working life

Some people think it's all entertainment:
receptions, dinners, visits to playcentres,

cocktail parties, laying foundation stones,
scissoring ribbons, sporting occasions.

I call it hard work: oily hands grasping,
smarmy grins, slippery speeches. And

the only jokes worth hearing are your own.
After a while the only people you meet

are spongers, toadies, lickspittles —
the functionaries of self-advancement.

They get in your hair, under your feet,
up your nose. Why do I stick at it, then?

Simple. It cost me my soul to get to the top
and I can't bear to step off.

18   Lack of sleep

I believe what I hear from informers
and trust eyes at the back of my head.
I make no secret of it. Public decency
depends on a fear of being found out.

Talk anti-state smut, scrawl anarchy
on the city walls, think political filth,
and be sure I'll find out.
Someone will always tell.

The glint in an eye can betray you.
Pillows gather whispers in the night.
Your laughter can be deciphered.
I am always awake, watching, listening.

No one can complain it doesn't work.
The nudes in the galleries wear figleaves;
kissing in public is restricted;
the poets have been liquidated.

You don't get these wise social reforms
without that abstinence from choice that rips
into the flesh. Its name is Authority.
It will only be when the people advance

at last towards reliable self-discipline
that I might at last get a good night's rest.
No wonder I often twitch. It's a sign
of the great strain of repressing you.

19　A musical question

Every policy attracts squawkers.
The better the law, the louder
the noise. Sometimes the clamour
is like the screaming of pigs
in a slaughterhouse.

New complaints flood in.
Fools shriek: 'TIBERIUS — YOU TYRANT!'
— though they wouldn't know what
the word meant if they fell into it
while making blood puddings.

When once I lived afraid
for my life, nobody heard me squeal:
'AUGUSTUS — YOU BUTCHER!' I made
the best of each day I had left
to clean up on musical theory.

While I still had time I wanted
the answer to one thing: in a world
like an abattoir — how come the secret
sovereignty of sweet voices?
What song did the Sirens sing?

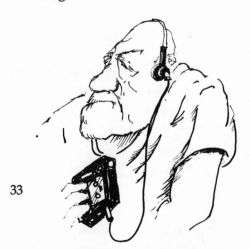

20   Ministerial appointments

A Cabinet of yes-men?
Eunuchs? Nobodies? Yobbos?

I don't agree. I think
they'd all get jobs

in the cruel world outside
scraping the bird-dirt

out of cuckoo-clocks.
Men of great worth.

I need them
to carry out instructions,

observe the correct procedures
and never ask policy questions.

That's the absolute truth.
It has nothing to do

with the way I enjoy
the political view

as I gaze over their heads,
or the way their inferiority

enhances my own prestige.
The magnificent triviality

of such lives shall outlast granite.
They shall always be known

as the Men of Tiberius
in the Age of Rome.

21   Absolute truth

They keep misunderstanding me:
when Emperors chisel phrases
such as Absolute Truth into marble,
they mean neither absolute nor truth.
Run your fingers along the stone scars:
the words are promises.

Just as when a priest raises
his pink palms from his vestments
and says God Exists, he is not talking
about God or existence, he is discussing
pinkness, the gold embroideries,
his promises.

Or when the general orders you to die
for your country he is promising
nothing more than that he can refashion
an instinct for self-preservation
into a wish to murder a stranger
from another land.

They keep misunderstanding me:
when Emperors carve promises of truth
into thin air, this is not an illusion.
I have never embroidered.
I speak in absolutes. They exist.
You can die for them.

22   Liberal deficiencies

These wispy liberals
with soggy eyes
and limp grey smiles
drive me crazy.
What right have they got
to a monopoly of conscience?

Who could claim
a bigger or more erect
conscience than myself?
I embrace the people.
I encourage them to be open.
I uplift them.

Positive thinking
and direct action
do the trick. The last
thing my subjects need
is all this wishy-washy
claptrap about deficiencies.

The trouble with liberals is
they confuse their private
lack with public need:
they muddle not being able
to raise one with the freedom
to talk about it.

23 The learning process

Exile brings two gifts:
(1) it concentrates the mind on home
and (2) you learn how everything fits.

Each shift of the wind smells
of the old city. Curtains tremble.
A door swings open. Wood smoke,

bread, garlic, lamb. Red wine.
A feast I held five years ago.
In exile, nostalgia is life.

Memory talks. It rubs musk
on you at night, climbs into bed,
takes your hand, instructs

you where to touch, when to connect,
how to make the separations.
It classifies the year of every scent

of lust, duplicity, ambition.
Exile makes you a political connoisseur,
gives you the status of Opposition.

You become the Alternative, the Future.
Never again will you know the same prestige.
Of Authority's sixty-nine postures

you have selected the most leisurely, supple.
You wait. Relax. Sniff the roses. No hurry.
The perfect moment is about to couple

with your destiny. Meanwhile, the days pass
and people change. They become transparent.
No more snuffling to guess

at motives; just gaze into their innermost
workings. The defects astonish you.
You learn there is no one to trust.

Friends must soon be liquidated. You smile —
you still call them Friends. Sentiment is not
corrupted, even by Opposition and exile.

24   Tiberius on the rocks

Fall on my bosom, love,
said she.
Laugh then leap
and fly to me.

Cock-a-hoop
I dived ahead,
but found my fun
cocked up instead.

Between two rocks
her heart resides.
I never laughed
yet split my sides.

25 Hoop-la

The shape of signatures
obsesses me. Stars, ovals,

squares, diamonds, triangles,
rhombs, tetragons, trapeziums.

Flourishes, points, bulges,
lines of force, sloppiness.

The geometry of personality.
So much pretension packed

into such small signs,
such tricky slogans. They are all

too self-assertive for my liking,
too exaggerated and immodest.

My favourite private sport
is to play hoop-la with signatures.

I imagine them as prizes.
Carefully I draw rings about them.

I win them. The man whose name
I circle is out of the game.

26　The Chinese waiter

Sometimes, sick of official lunches,
lamb chops and stodge, I'd send a secretary
to fetch fish and chips or disguise myself
and go Chinese — nothing quite like
a fresh plate of crunchy won tons.

My favourite eating place was just around
the corner. The best won tons in town.
How they crackled when I bit — the sound
of doors clicking shut, keys rattling in locks,
bones breaking. Scrumptious.

Then one night they vanished from the menu.
'No won tons?' I asked. 'Why's that?'
The Chinese waiter gave me a look I'd only
seen before in a mirror. Flicking a crumb
with a napkin, he announced: 'No reason given.'

God and Caesar speak like that. Same phrase.
Same tone. Brilliant. Students of politics,
investigating the genius of Tiberius,
could do no better than put aside the menu
and listen closely to the waiter.

27 Tiberius reflects

When I was young I used to steal up
on mirrors to see if I could catch
my face dreaming. Now I never have time.

In between circuses, orgies and executions
there's only the odd moment
to receive ambassadors, dedicate shrines,

make a snap inspection of the treasury,
summon a barber to give me a quick shave,
and snatch a sandwich.

I live on the run, stumbling further
and further behind. I'm in so much
of a hurry, there's no time to think.

And as for faces in mirrors, I haven't
accosted mine in one for years. It has now
got to the point where I'm frightened to look.

What if last week's face is still catching up
with me? That bloodshot eye? That rictus
of lust? What if there's no reflection?

28 Imperial diversions

It is an old trick of government
to stage imperial diversions
whenever the rabble gets stroppy.

Nothing like levelling a foreign city
to the ground or a superb massacre
to repair the national pride.

Victory parades lift the civic spirit.
Our meanest beggars look down
on the slaves our conquests crop,

and the loot our debtors glimpse
as I cart it off to the treasury
lets them dream they're millionaires.

That is one of the chief differences
between Roman civilisation
and the barbarians: our official

strategies have purpose and art;
theirs are a matter of improvisation.
Naturally, I have a joke for it as I

send in my ambassadors with threats:
'The world is a woman. I am her seducer.
Ergo, I conduct foreign affairs.'

29 Consider Rome as a brain

What is happening to Rome? they ask.
Our city vanishes. We wake in the morning
to the sound of hammers and cascading walls.
The streets sink beneath rubble. The dust
falls in a slow drizzle. Memories drown.

My answer is: that's the price of progress —
if you don't like it, pack up, leave town,
live in a cave. It's your choice. On
the other hand, if you fancy bold statements,
grand gestures and a stake in our high-rise

destiny, don't moan when I smash your antique
hovels to the ground to build offices. And don't
let me hear you grizzle about me living it up
on Capri while you suffer — as is your due —
such eloquent benefits of our profound capacity

for Latin compression as 'pulverisation'.
Consider Rome as a brain. I smooth the bumps,
obliterate a tumbledown collective recollection,
I create a tabula rasa. On it I redesign dreams.
Think, citizens. Each day is a new beginning.

30 Money matters

Over a drink, the courageous wastrels
call me General Herringbone, Lord Hoarder,
Prince Pinchgut, King Skinflint. Very funny.
My spies are so ashamed I have to torture

them to confess my latest nickname.
How they piss themselves to part
with painful jokes comparing my largesse
with the generosity of a cat's arse

or confide to the castrating device
songs like the one that goes 'Tiberius
the parsimonious', then rhymes nefarious
with penurious — disfigurements of the niceties

of prosody I repay with long and savage
mutilations. Mostly I feel contempt.
Such sniggerings don't matter.
It's the ingratitude I resent,

the blind wrong. While they fling
their money around like drunken pimps,
nudging and winking, I shower them with hope,
imperial causes, destiny. I have skimped

and scraped to secure for them a future
in which they shall celebrate
the fortune I've salted away in the vaults.
When my will is read and they dislocate

their jaws reciting my million millions
there'll be no more cheap laughs.
Proud to be Romans — Caesar's men — they'll
think they're worth something at last.

31   Caesar at the brain factory

I have always been devoted to the cause
of higher education. A literate, numerate
workforce is the prime resource of modern
industry and commerce. No point in building

warehouses or office blocks without
an inexhaustible supply of trained talent.
That's why I'm sometimes heard to complain
about the waste of money in the universities.

What's the use of courses in history,
philosophy, classics and such, when what we need
are accountants, economists, statisticians,
lawyers, actuaries, managers, auditors,

programmers and informed businessmen? Not
so much a university, more a brain factory.
We also have the problem of succession:
the next Caesar will need new skills — it's no

task for an amateur. How else to guide the state
than with a solid background in double-
cross bookkeeping? Privateering enterprise,
ledger-demain — that's the true education.

32 Predicament

There are two ways to get into one:
you muck things up by exercise of will
or you submit to fate.

I have heard them called nomination
and predetermination, freedom
and necessity, choice and compulsion.

The labels don't help. Between them
I become a grape in a tun, mashed
by the toes of a drunken winemaker,

an olive in the press, a carcass
on a butcher's block as the knife falls.
Caesar and God live in a torture chamber

of contradictions. The walls keep closing
in on us. There are things we cannot do.
We cannot do wrong or be in error

or sleep under newspapers in a shop doorway.
Soldiers and priests confine us.
We can destroy cities, perform miracles,

we can decide to live on Capri. Yet once,
when we chose the woman we loved, we had
to cast her off and graft our line to royalty.

Dynastic requirements contrived to outwit
free will. The people call us tyrants.
They make us weep. We are Rome's slaves.

33   Swearing in print

You'll notice I seldom swear
in print. My thoughts are too
violent, too foul for that.
Sissies write smutty words.
Still trying to shock mum.

The most obscene word I can
think of — and my hand trembles
to connect its marks across
this page — is Justice. It bleeds,
writhes, howls. It reeks of iron,

red-hot, smoking on flesh.
It opens your bowels. I can't
stand all these jellyfish —
poets and novelists — wobbling on
with their political filth.

When I catch them at it, I apply
corrections to their consonants
and vowels. I offer them Justice.
A healthy state purges language.
I am just a glorified literary critic.

34 Reasons of state

Timorous? Tiberius?
They call me the hero of inaction.

Balls. It is simpler to say yes,
much easier to act,

less trouble to agree
and more pleasant to plunge on —

forwards, urgently, with trumpets.
Where? Probably nowhere. In circles.

I earned my old notoriety comfortably,
tackling problems, making history.

No hesitation. Straight in. No effort.
Just as I now labour

for a reputation for paralysis.
It is hard work. I sweat in bed.

Occasionally, I even
slip back into old habits:

e.g., this morning I left for Rome,
events were begging me

to say yes, act, agree
and charge ahead with them.

Then a black cat stepped across
my path. Before I could counter

by crossing my fingers
and summoning a white horse

it fixed its amber eyes
on me and screamed:

'Tiberius! Timorous!'
Naturally I turned back.

Superstition is the lubricant
of political will.

It eases the big decisions,
saves effort.

The black cat and I
know what it's all about.

35   A letter from home

To be an exile
is of little interest.
People leave. The reasons

are too simple.
They are always irrefutable.
We know ourselves too well.

A train is just about
to depart. There is a ticket.
A friend waves.

No one sits
in a hotel at the edge
of the desert and asks

'How did I get here?'
unless they have first
emptied a bottle of pills

into their gin.
Exile is too commonplace.
It is a condition.

To return from exile
is to offer too many complex
explanations. There is always

one more motive
one more complication
to add to your confusion.

You attempt plain answers.
They tend to contradict
each other. In the end

you discover the words
cancel each other out.
You have never been away.

36   A soldier's tale

It was in the East.
One of those migrant people
who crawl round the rotten scrag-ends
of empire, like a necklace of maggots.

Barbarians. Yet they had managed somehow
to build huts, clothe themselves,
and rub clay to represent
beasts, birds and fat women.

They became a footnote to Rome's
requirements. Our policy was to make
the border safe. They had to go.
We killed them, babes and all.

A year later we found one man
in a cave. He had escaped
the carnage. A specimen
of a species we had thought extinct.

The intellect of isolation
inspires me. I questioned him.
I had him flagellated to help him think.
He answered in splutters, hisses

and screeches. The whining buzz of a blowfly.
His people had been too new
to the province. None of his neighbours
understood a single discord.

And, of course, he grasped no Latin.
He was the only being on Earth
who understood his own language.
In the end, that made us brothers.

37 Tiberius observes the master of mosaics

You can tell
he is thinking of something else.
The lips talk to dreams.
A force outside him
decides the way he moves.

The curtains spread then fall.
A wind catches at his hands,
and as he sways then tilts
a glazed shard spills from him
into its exact place.

Faces surface from the walls.
Each time the wind breathes
a foot kicks free,
an eye opens from sleep.
The inhabitants of bricks

rise from their caked darkness
and join us — here
where we talk to dreams
and walls recite
their memories of the clay.

38 Tiberius recites a political parable

Darkness hunted the Sun, who dropped
everything and ran — and just
managed to escape through a crack
at the end of the last street in town.

The golden slavedriver's rule was over.
People were jubilant and began to kiss.
The new regime had promised them
the freedom of the night.

And, indeed, was not the first act
of Darkness to strike away the shadows
the Sun had chained to their ankles?
There were now no restrictions.

Everyone was happy until they noticed
that Darkness had made them blind.
That was not part of the bargain.
'We want to see again!' they yelled.

Darkness quoted: 'Give and take —
that's the new philosophy.
You want pleasure —
you have to make sacrifices.'

It was so black that people could not
read or write. They could only dream.
They had to send emissaries of sleep
to beg the old tyrant to return.

39 Walking

When Drusus died in the far north
he rode home on a chariot.
I chose to walk.

His corpse came back in comfort.
My feet were bruised
and blistered.

Such is the way of true grief.
There is no dodging
the heart's absurdity.

When I think of my brother
I hear the rasp of chariot wheels
and the jangle of harness.

The hooves that hauled him to Rome
clapped the same rhythm as girls
dancing in the brothels.

40 Definitions of beauty

Beauty. I have seen sculptors
measuring it. Ears, noses, elbows,
ankles and backsides. The perfect form,
unblemished harmony, flawless proportion.

Like tailors, they try to get the fit
exactly right. Beauty. The naked body
wearing the air about it, and the light,
like a new kit of clothes.

I think of it only as flesh.
Sauces. Beauty. Spices. Juices.
I close my eyes and taste it.
Edible.

Running a hand down the thigh
of a statue, I hear my tongue
slam against the back of my teeth.
Foraging. Saliva loosens my lips.

Beauty exists even in black night.
It has syllables of smell
and flavour. Hot meat. Steam rattling
the lid of the pot. Gravy. Beauty.

41   A lesson in politics

My good friend, Sejanus,
washes his feet in the Tiber.
His hands are clean.

No man, no woman,
can go higher than Sejanus.
He is an example to us all.

Until tonight
he ruled in my name.
I put him in charge,

trusted him, patted his back,
gave him my son's widow.
Then the news came —

'Sejanus commissions statues
to himself. Bulls are slaughtered
to Sejanus.'

Tonight he washes his feet
in the Tiber. His hands
are clean. His body

lies on the rocks
and the river wipes away
the spit of a thousand throats.

He exudes a trail of slime,
like a slug. Sejanus,
my good friend, hail!

42 Playing for the team

It's all right complaining
about the codes of conduct
we drill into the young —

the way we elevate hearty
brutalities into rules of honour
and convert lying, cheating

and spying into principles
of practical ethics — but stop
for a moment and think of Rome as

an island in demented seas,
a fortress in a dark forest,
the one civilised eye

at the centre of the storm,
a torch at night,
the beak above the worm.

If we go soft, the barbarians
bite back and the world becomes
a bloodbath. We can't have that —

it has taken a developed
sense of discipline to achieve
Roman refinements and we are not

going to chuck it all away just
because a few spoilt children
say it's not fair. Civilisation

is a chariot borne by Culture
and the Law. It is designed
to keep balance

while moving forwards.
Fairness distorts its purpose,
perverts its elegance —

the precise proportions — and impairs
the running order. Team spirit
and shared assumptions provide

the motive power. Without labouring
the metaphor, one could assert,
confidently, that civilisation transports

human defects into my hard and fast rule.
This function must always prevail.
How else do we explain the driver?

43 News from the distance

News from the distance
says there has been an outbreak
of delusions of grandeur.
Every tin-pot backblocks campsite

in the East is throwing up
usurpers, heirs to lost thrones,
emperors, excellencies, highnesses,
majesties, and now a King

of Kings. I am inclined
to doubt the reports.
News is contagious: a good story
catches on in one place

then goes the full round
of the provinces. The further
it travels the worse it gets.
The next sensations are sure

to be rabid republicanism
or a bad bout of religious mania.
There is nothing more certain
than that tomorrow my runners

will arrive breathless
with the same yarns that every year
strain our imperial communications.
In caves beyond the walls

of their obscure towns at the world's end
misfits and dreamers are busy
plotting the revival of old hoaxes.
I've heard them all. Miracle-workers

owe great thanks to the Empire:
they claim their day of glory only because
the information gets through.
The real miracle is Rome.

44 Upright and clean

Never depend on a friend.
Place the full weight
of your trust on one
and the next thing you know

you're arse over elbow.
Integrity has as many slippery
tip-you-ups as a cake
of soap in a bath.

Betrayal is ace
when it comes to reliability.
And it comes in two sizes:
giant, with 10% extra squeak,

and the economy package,
the one that mocks faith,
tips you the wink, and
lets you in on the joke.

Without betrayal you'd never
rule Rome. It takes the dirt
out of politics. Everyone
knows where they stand.

45   A final message

I was offered a cushion
yesterday, and I got it stuffed
right down my throat. As if
it hasn't been hard enough

to communicate from the other
side of the grave, I have
had to mutter through a mouth
full of feathers. So listen

carefully, I have something
of great importance to get
across to those of you who woke
this morning and moaned

when you found you were subjects
of someone called Caligula.
Before suffocating an Emperor
the first rule is

always knock at the gates
of the palace and ask:
'By the way, who's next
in line to the throne?'